D0857057

SOLVING MYSTERIES WITH SCIENCE

Mermaids

LORI HILE

Raintree

Chicago, Illinois

Edited by Adam Miller and Abby Colich
Designed by Marcus Bell
Original illustrations (pages 7, 11,15) © Chris King
 2013
All other original illustrations © Capstone Global
 Library
Illustrated by Chris King and HL Studios
Picture research by Mica Brancic
Originated by Capstone Global Library, Ltd.
Printed in China by Leo Paper Group

17 16 15 14 13 12
10 9 8 7 6 5 4 3 2 1

**Library of Congress Cataloging-in-Publication
Data**
Hile, Lori.
Mermaids / Lori Hile.—1st ed.
p. cm.—(Solving mysteries with science)
Includes bibliographical references and index.
ISBN 978-1-4109-4989-9 (hb)—ISBN 978-1-4109-
4994-3 (pb)
1. Mermaids—Juvenile literature. I. Title.

GR910.H54 2013
398.21—dc23   2012012738

Acknowledgments

The author and publisher are grateful to the following
for permission to reproduce copyright material:
akg-images: pp. 33 (Erich Lessing), 35 (Erich Lessing);
Alamy: pp. 25 (© Martin Strmiska), 31 (© AF
archive), 38 (© Corbis Bridge/Zena Holloway), 43
(© BL Images Ltd); Corbis: pp. 18 (© Blue Lantern
Studio), 21 (Reuters/© Pilar Olivares), 22 bottom
(© Fiona Rogers), 24 (© Bettmann), 26–27 (©
Bettmann), 29 (© Stuart Westmorland), 30 bottom
(dpa/© Hinrich Baesemann); Getty Images: pp.
23 (Photographer's Choice/David Sutherland), 41
(Mark Kolbe); Juan Cabana: p. 39; Nature Picture
Library: p. 32 (Rotman/© Bruce Rasner); Science
Photo Library: p. 26 (Paul D Stewart); Shutterstock:
pp. 4 (© Lafoto), 5 top (© Drakonova), 5 bottom (©
Andrea Danti), 19 (© Liliya Kulianionak), 20 left (©
Alexander Raths), 20 middle (© Vita Khorzhevska), 20
right (© Edyta Pawlowska), 22 top (© DenisNata), 30
top (© Nataliia Antonova), 36 (© Lynea), 40 (© Sam
DCruz); The Bridgeman Art Library: pp. 34 (Private
Collection/Photo © Bonhams, London, UK), 37
(Guildhall Library, City of London), 42 (The Stapleton
Collection/Private Collection).

Cover photograph of a mermaid reproduced with
permission from Getty Images (The Image Bank/
Steve Williams Photo).

Every effort has been made to contact copyright
holders of any material reproduced in this book. Any
omissions will be rectified in subsequent printings if
notice is given to the publisher.

All the Internet addresses (URLs) given in this book
were valid at the time of going to press. However, due
to the dynamic nature of the Internet, some addresses
may have changed, or sites may have changed or
ceased to exist since publication. While the author
and publisher regret any inconvenience this may
cause readers, no responsibility for any such changes
can be accepted by either the author or the publisher.

Contents

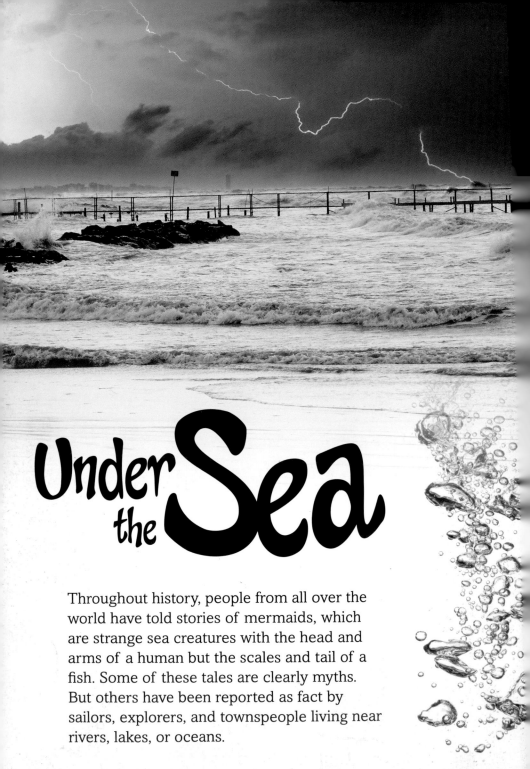

Under the Sea

Throughout history, people from all over the world have told stories of mermaids, which are strange sea creatures with the head and arms of a human but the scales and tail of a fish. Some of these tales are clearly myths. But others have been reported as fact by sailors, explorers, and townspeople living near rivers, lakes, or oceans.

Could mermaids really exist?

In the first part of this book, we will follow some exciting eyewitness sightings. In the second part of the book, we will use the scientific method (see page 19) to examine these accounts and help answer the question: Could mermaids really exist?

Mermaid mythology:
Mermen

Not all mermaids are female. Male mer-creatures, usually called "mermen," have also been sighted and featured in stories. In fact, one of the first recorded mermaid myths is about a Babylonian god named Oannes, with the upper body of a man and the tail of a fish. Triton, a Greek god of the sea, was also depicted as half-man, half-fish. While mermaids are usually described as beautiful creatures, with long, blonde locks and rosy cheeks, mermen often have ugly features including green teeth, pig eyes, and long, red noses.

FISH-WOMAN

Lightning flashed over the North Sea as sheets of rain pelted the waters below. Wild winds whipped white-capped waves sideways, sweeping a strange, sleeping creature into Zuiderzee Bay, off the coast of Holland (in the present-day Netherlands). With nothing to cling to, the creature washed across the bay and into Lake Purmer, in the village of Edam.

Normally, a stone wall called a dike blocked the bay from flooding the town, but the storm had carved a huge hole in the dike.

TRAPPED IN THE LAKE

After the winds quieted, townsmen fixed the hole in the dike, unaware that they were also trapping the creature in the lake. Much of the village remained underwater, so several young women sailed across the flooded fields in little boats to milk their cows, which were grazing on dry patches of land. As they neared the water's edge, one of the girls screamed. There, caught in the mud, lay a creature unlike any she had ever seen.

TANGLED

Covered only by a tangle of moss and seaweed, the creature had the face and upper body of a woman. But instead of legs, the creature's body curved into the tail of a fish!

CAPTURED!

The young women hovered over the creature, believing she was dead.

Then, suddenly, the creature's eyelids fluttered open, revealing a pair of wild eyes.

Trembling, the girls rushed back to their boats and fled for home.

The next day, two bold girls rowed back to the lake and pulled the squirming fish-woman on board. They covered her in a blanket and paddled her back to Edam. There, they gently removed the moss and seaweed from her body and dressed her in women's clothing. They fed the fish-woman food from their own cupboards and tried to teach her to speak. But the creature would only utter strange singsong sounds.

GRAZING AT THE LAKE

The fish-woman enjoyed baths, and when the young girls got busy with their daily chores, she would wriggle her way toward the lake—only to encounter a guard who was stationed there to prevent her from jumping in. Soon, the fish-woman learned to spin wool into yarn, like an ordinary townswoman. But she seldom smiled and was often seen gazing sadly toward the sea.

After she died, the strange creature was given a proper burial, and a statue of a mermaid was built in her honor next to the Purmer Gate in Edam. On it, these words were printed:

"This statue was erected [built] in memory of what had been caught in Lake Purmer in the year 1403."

For many years, the mermaid statue remained by the gate, looking out at the lake.

CAPTURED: THE MERMAID OF AMBOINA

As Dutch sailors neared the South Asian island of Borneo in the late 1700s, they were startled to see a fish with a body as long as a woman's! After catching the creature in their nets, they could see the fish had webbed fingers and two small breasts.

The creature's skinny body began with an oval-shaped head and ended with a long, blue tail. Mystified, the sailors placed the odd, quivering creature into a tub of water.

The sailors kept careful watch on the creature and sometimes heard it whimper like a mouse. Believing it hungry, they offered it small fish, shells, and crab to eat. But the creature refused and eventually died, after four days and seven hours.

ENCOUNTERS WITH MERFOLK

British sea captain Richard Whitbourne stood on the shore of St. John's harbor in Newfoundland, Canada, in 1610, gazing out at the sea, when he saw something swimming swiftly toward him. Was it a woman? It had a round face with delicate features and what appeared to be long, blue strands of hair streaming past a cream-colored neck.

When the creature drew within an arm's length of the shore, Whitbourne retreated. Although he had fearlessly fought against a powerful Spanish army and commanded ships across the vast Atlantic Ocean, he had never encountered a woman like this before—one who appeared out of the mists of the sea.

When he stepped back, the figure dived into the waves and abruptly switched directions, paddling away from Whitbourne and toward his ship, anchored out in the harbor. This gave Whitbourne the opportunity to observe the creature's shoulders and back, which were as milky-white and smooth as those of a human. But from the mid-section down, the creature's body was long and pointed, like an arrow.

Could it be a mermaid?

Whitbourne's servant, William Hawkridge, and another crew member watched in amazement as the creature wriggled toward their ship. But their awe turned to panic when the creature propped her hands on the side of the boat, preparing to lunge at them.

HIT ON THE HEAD

In fear, one of the men grabbed an oar and struck the creature on the head, sending her spiraling back into the chilly Atlantic waters. But the creature did not give up easily. Instead, she swam toward other boats, causing the sailors to flee for dry land. Whitbourne later described the incident. He wrote: "This, I suppose, was a mermaid."

SALTY SAILORS

As English explorer Henry Hudson sailed through a group of islands north of Russia in 1608, two members of his crew spied an odd-looking woman in the water. They called up other crew members, and by the time the men arrived, the figure was hovering by the side of the ship, staring at the men.

As waves bumped the boat, the creature flipped over, allowing the men to see her from the navel up. She was as large as a man, but she had the breasts of a woman and long, black hair cascading down her ivory back. When she dived back into the water, the men were amazed to see that she had a tail like a porpoise, dotted with speckles.

A CARIBBEAN CREATURE

In 1614, another English captain, John Smith, noticed a lovely lady swimming gracefully near the Caribbean coast. He found her large eyes, short nose, long ears, and green hair attractive and he even experienced pangs of love. As he leaned down from his ship to talk with the uncommon woman, Smith was shocked to see that, from the waist down, the woman "gave way to the fish!"

MERMAID MYTHOLOGY: MELUSINE

According to legend, mermaids can live on land for a while. But for most, the call of the sea is too powerful, and they soon long to return to the waters from which they came. In the famous French folktale of Melusine, the son of a French count meets the beautiful Melusine near the seashore. He asks her to marry him, and she agrees, under one condition: that she spend Saturdays completely alone in their castle.

They get married, and the man keeps his promise—until one Saturday, when he peeks through the keyhole into her dressing room. He sees his wife splashing in the bathtub and realizes that the lower part of her body has transformed into the huge, blue tail of a fish! Melusine soon finds out that he has spied on her. Because of his betrayal, she leaves her human family and returns to the sea.

MODERN MERMAIDS

Eight-year-old Catherine Loynachan was herding cattle on her father's farm near the sea in Corphin, Scotland. But as she turned the cattle toward home, she spotted an odd creature on a rock near the seaside. At first, she thought it was a little boy with long, dark hair. But then she noticed that the creature's shoulders were spotted, and the rest of its body tapered into the tail of a fish! Just then, the creature slid on its belly into the sea and vanished under the water. It resurfaced about 6 yards (5.5 meters) away, then swung around to face the shore.

Catherine was able to clearly see its face, which was white and small. Its hands were also small, like those of a young boy. It laid one hand on a rock and used the other to feverishly rub its chest, as if scrubbing itself.

After Catherine and the creature peered at one another for a moment, the animal turned and disappeared under the sea.

Catherine hurried home to tell her parents, because she thought the creature could be a boy who had fallen off a boat. She returned to the shore with her parents, but there was no sign of the boy-fish.

A SECOND SIGHTING

A man named John McIsaac spotted a mermaid with an almost identical description later that same day, October 18, 1811, on a rock near the shore in Corphin.

A MERMAID IN THE 1900s

In 1967, a ferryboat filled with passengers was traveling between Vancouver and the city of Victoria, on Vancouver Island, in Canada. On this trip full of beautiful scenery, travelers often observe wildlife, including bald eagles, seals, and orcas (killer whales).

But this time, as the ferry entered Active Pass, a narrow passage between islands, several passengers were surprised to see an unfamiliar creature sitting on some rocks.

As they moved closer, they could see that the figure had long, blonde hair and the lower body of a porpoise!

The mermaid was calmly munching on a piece of salmon. A plane buzzed overhead around the same time, and a passenger snapped a picture of the creature. It was published, along with news of the sighting, in a local newspaper.

A MODERN MERMAID

Shlomo Cohen was beachcombing with friends near Kiryat Yam, Israel, in 2009, when he saw a woman sprawled on the sand at a strange angle.

At first, Cohen thought she was just another sunbather. But as he approached the woman, she leapt into the water, and Cohen could see that she had a tail like a dolphin!

A MILLION-DOLLAR MERMAID?

Soon the town was flooded with sightings of the unusual fish-woman. Around sunset, the half-girl, half-fish would appear and perform a series of acrobatic tricks before vanishing into the waves. News of the mermaid drew crowds of people with cameras to the beach, all of them hoping to catch a glimpse. The town even offered a $1 million reward to anyone who could prove the mermaid's existence.

A MERMAID MIRAGE

When 16-year-old Cleo Rosin neared the Zambezi River in Zimbabwe to collect drinking water with her mother in 1951, she spied an island that she'd never seen before. But even more amazing was what she saw sitting on the island's edge. It was a beautiful white woman with long, black hair, completely naked. Cleo called out to her mother, who was filling buckets with water. "Mother, look at the woman over there!" But her mother warned Cleo to keep quiet. "Shhh," she said. "Look away." But Cleo had already seen the lower part of the woman's body, which curved into a fish tail. Still, Cleo turned her eyes away, and when she glanced up again, the woman vanished.

The Evolution of Mermaids

Almost every culture and country has stories about mermaids. And for years, mermaids seemed just as likely to exist as other creatures from legends, such as unicorns, dragons, or fairies. With the introduction of modern science in the 1700s, people started to question the idea of mermaids. But that did not stop people from spotting them. Most of these people have sworn that their accounts are true.

Portrait of a mermaid

Mermaids have long been thought to possess certain characteristics, including:

Special gifts: It is said that some mermaids have the ability to grant wishes, tell the future, or shift shapes.

Beauty: Mermaids are often pictured lying on rocks while holding a mirror or combing their long, flowing locks.

Enchanting singing voices: Some people say mermaids attract sailors to rocky shores with their lovely melodies.

Could mermaids really exist? Or is there another explanation? In this section of the book, we will use the scientific method (see the box) to help explain the mystery of mermaids.

► Are mermaids creatures of fact or fantasy?

The scientific method

Good investigators follow the scientific method when they need to establish and test a theory. The scientific method has five basic steps:

1. Make observations (comments based on studying something closely).
2. Do some background research.
3. Form a testable hypothesis. This is basically a prediction or "educated guess" to explain the observations.
4. Conduct experiments or find evidence to support the hypothesis.
5. After thinking carefully about the evidence, draw conclusions.

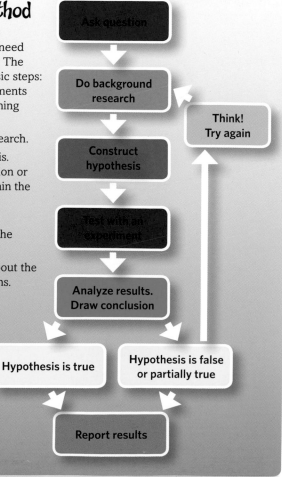

Ask question

Do background research

Construct hypothesis

Test with an experiment

Analyze results. Draw conclusion

Think! Try again

Hypothesis is true

Hypothesis is false or partially true

Report results

Mermaids: The missing link?

Could mermaids be our long-lost relatives? Ancient Greek thinker Anaximander believed that all life started in water. He claimed that, as dry land emerged, certain animals learned to live on the land and, over time, lost their scales and fins.

English naturalist Charles Darwin built on this idea when he proposed his theory of evolution in 1859. And if all creatures evolved (developed) from sea animals, it is not hard to imagine that there might, at one time, have been a creature that was part-human and part-fish, like a mermaid. This creature could have been a "missing link" between sea creatures and humans.

Searching for mermaids

In 1872, the British government sent a boat called the HMS *Challenger* to test Darwin's theory of evolution. One of its goals was to search the seas for evidence of "missing links" between animals. By 1895, scientists had found evidence for "missing links" between many sea creatures, but there was no fossil evidence for half-fish, half-human animals like mermaids.

In his 1871 book *The Descent of Man*, Darwin suggested that humans had descended from relatives of apes, not directly from sea creatures. Although his theory was debated for decades, it is widely accepted by scientists today.

▲ Could mermaids be the link between fish and humans?

Shiloh Pepin: A little mermaid

Like many children, Shiloh Pepin loved swimming, playing at the playground, and dancing. But unlike most children, Shiloh resembled a mermaid. She suffered from a very rare medical condition called sirenomelia, also known as Mermaid Syndrome, in which humans are born with their legs fused (attached) together like a mermaid's tail. Some people believe that sirenomelia might account for some mermaid sightings. But, sadly, most children suffering from this condition live no more than a few hours after birth. Shiloh, however, defied the odds. She lived for 10 years, until 2009.

▼ Milagros Cerron, pictured below, was born with a rare condition called sirenomelia, in which her legs are joined together, like a mermaid's.

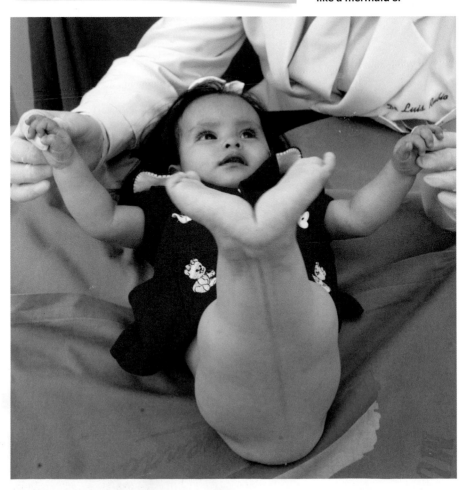

Aquatic ape hypothesis

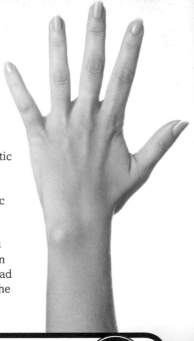

Place one of your hands in front of you, with your knuckles facing up, then spread it open as wide as you can. Look at the skin between your fingers. Can you see how it resembles the webbing on the foot of a frog or duck? This is just one reason some scientists have proposed that humans are more closely related to aquatic (sea) animals than apes. Another reason is that humans are much less hairy than apes. And many hairless mammals, like elephants and rhinoceroses, have aquatic relatives.

This hypothesis, called the aquatic ape hypothesis, says that humans descended from a type of ape that lived on the shores of lakes. Since these creatures would have had both aquatic and ape-like features, perhaps they were the creatures that we call "mermaids"?

Myth-buster

Aquatic ape hypothesis debunked

Humans do have some features in common with aquatic animals, but most of these traits can be explained by standard theories of evolution. For instance, humans may have less body hair than apes because humans mated with other humans with very little hair. But the biggest blow to the aquatic ape hypothesis is that no fossils of an "aquatic ape" have ever been found.

A real-life mermaid

There is a woman in New Zealand named Nadya Vassey who could be mistaken for a mermaid. Due to a medical condition, her legs were removed when she was an infant. But as an adult, she asked Weta Workshop, a famous prop and costume company, to make her a mermaid tail. She used it to swim in a recent triathlon, which is a sports event with swimming, cycling, and running competitions.

▶ Some humans use props or costumes to dress as mermaids.

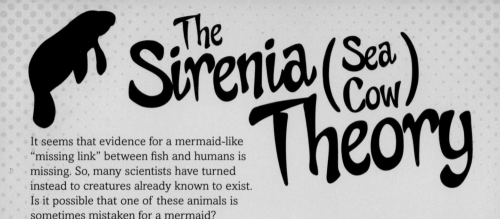

The Sirenia (Sea Cow) Theory

It seems that evidence for a mermaid-like "missing link" between fish and humans is missing. So, many scientists have turned instead to creatures already known to exist. Is it possible that one of these animals is sometimes mistaken for a mermaid?

The sea cow

At first, sea cows may seem like an unlikely candidate. Instead of slender, graceful figures, sea cows have large, cucumber-shaped bodies and weigh over eight times as much as the average human. At 13 feet (4 meters), they are also over twice as long. Their skin is rough and gray, and instead of arms, they have rounded flippers.

But some scientists are so sure sea cows are the "mermaids" that have been reported that they have named this group of mammals "sirenians," after the sea-dwelling creatures known as sirens in ancient Greek myths. Sirenians include three species of manatees and one species of dugong.

▼ Some scientists believe that people who spot mermaids are really seeing a manatee, a form of sea cow. Do you think you would ever mistake a big, bulky manatee for a mermaid?

Sea cows and mermaids: Separated at birth?

Mermaids and sea cows (manatees or dugongs) do share some surprising similarities. As mammals, sea cows must occasionally rise to the surface to breathe air—and they do so headfirst, just like humans. Female manatees and dugongs have breasts and could resemble a woman, especially when they rise out of the water to suckle their young. Their short, paddle-like flippers allow sea cows to swim gracefully— and could even be mistaken for short human arms. Since sea cows feed on sea grass in shallow waters, they are also likely to be spotted by observers near the shore.

"There have been times when they come up out of the water and the light has been such that they did look like the head of a person."

—Scientist James Powell, on working with manatees

▶ Dugongs rise head first out of the water, just like humans.

From a distance, an untrained observer could perhaps mistake a sea cow for a mermaid. But what about a sailor, who spends his life at sea? Could he really believe that a big, bulky, bald manatee or a whiskered dugong was a beautiful mermaid? Maybe to a sailor in the 1600s it may not seem so crazy.

In the books

Imagine opening a science book and finding mermaids listed alongside other sea creatures like whales, dolphins, and shrimp. Until the mid-1700s, this is exactly what you might find in natural history books, which most explorers studied. Some explorers also read stories with mermaids, including classic tales like *The Odyssey*. In the story, from 800 BCE, Greek war hero Odysseus encounters sirens on his 10-year journey home.

▲ This illustration, from a 17th-century science book, includes pictures of Triton, a Greek god with the head of a man and the tail of a fish.

Uncharted territory

Before venturing into new territories, explorers extensively studied maps. But because much of the world was still unexplored, mapmakers often used their imaginations to fill in unknown areas. They drew pictures of oceans teeming with strange sea monsters and mermaids.

The power of desire

Now imagine that you have been sailing for several months on an unfamiliar sea. You are tired and miss your wife, girlfriend, or mother. Maybe it is getting dark, and you see a creature rise out of the water. You do not recognize the creature, but you see that it has the breasts of a woman…and the tail of a dolphin. It does not look exactly like the mermaid of myth, but it comes close. It fulfills your fantasy of finding a fantastic sea creature— and a female companion. So you decide to call it a mermaid. Plus, reporting a mermaid makes for a colorful sea story!

◄ An artist in the 1500s drew this depiction of the ocean, filled with strange sea animals.

Where do mermaids live?

Dugongs live in mild, shallow waters off the Indian Ocean, near Indonesia and Australia. Manatees make their homes in rivers and freshwater lakes in Florida, the coasts of the Caribbean and Brazil, and the Congo River in Africa. So sea cows might account for the mermaids spotted by explorers Christopher Columbus and John Smith, who were sailing along the tropical Caribbean coast.

But how do we explain the mermaid found near Holland's cold North Sea? Or the various sightings off the chilly coast of Scotland—or Newfoundland? Also, neither manatees nor dugongs live in the Mediterranean Sea near Greece or the ancient city of Babylon, the source of many mermaid myths. These sightings and stories require a different explanation.

In the land of giants

When Christopher Columbus first arrived in the "New World," he may have expected to encounter giants, pygmies (a race of short people), Amazons (a tribe of all-female warriors), and "dog-faced savages." That is how Cardinal Pierre d'Ailly described the other side of the world in *Imago Mundi*, Columbus's favorite book. Perhaps Columbus was inspired by visions of these fantastic creatures when he saw mermaids off the coast of the New World.

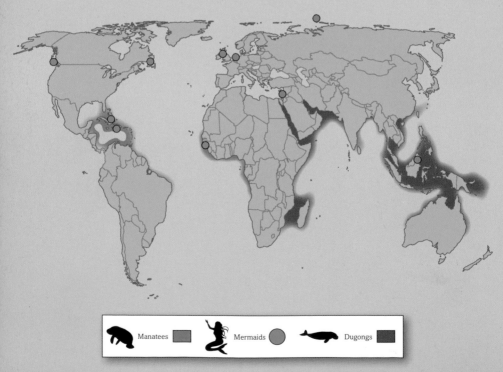

| Manatees ▬ | Mermaids ● | Dugongs ▬ |

▼ Since manatees swim close to shore, they are often injured by speed boats. But hopefully these real-life "mermaids" will continue to live on.

Could sirenians become extinct?

Because sea cows are so large, they have no natural predators (animals that hunt them). Yet all species of sea cow are now in danger of dying out. Why? Before hunting was banned in 1893, hundreds of thousands of manatees were killed for their meat, which was considered a treat to eat. But now manatees are much more likely to be seriously hurt or killed by collisions with motorboat propellers. The shrinking number of manatees could explain the shrinking number of "mermaid" sightings.

Seals and Other Creatures of the Sea

Sea cows cannot account for all mermaid sightings, but, luckily, there are lots of other creatures in the sea!

Could a whale, dolphin, or porpoise be mistaken for a mermaid? These mammals, called cetaceans, have mermaid-shaped tails. And their four flippers are bony, like human limbs. It is possible that some early mermaids—like one captured off the coast of Scotland in 887 CE, which measured 195 feet (59 meters)—were really whales. But most cetaceans have pointier heads than humans (or sea cows) and were probably familiar to early explorers.

▼ Like fish, seals have fins. But some of their gestures and expressions look almost human.

Seal sirens?

You are exhausted after a long journey when you hear a sweet song. You look to the nearby shore, where you see a creature with a round head, green eyes—and a flipper. Maybe the creature scratches its head. Is it a mermaid? Scientists say it is probably a seal.

Seals like to bask on rocks, where "mermaids" are often spotted. And unlike silent sea cows, seals can utter haunting musical notes, like the sirens of myths. Most seals are gray, but a few are pink or rust-colored, like some human skin. They have eyes of every shade and flexible flippers, which they use to wipe their heads or noses, like humans. But there is one problem. Since seals are often found lounging on beaches, they are usually recognized…as seals.

Mermaid mythology: Seal women

Could a woman be hidden under the skin of a seal? The ancient Greeks thought so—and so did the Irish, who called these creatures selkies. A variation on mermaids, selkies swam like seals in water but appeared as women on dry land, when they took off their skins.

▲ In this image from the film *Nim's Island*, a girl swims with a selkie.

Cryptozoology and other hypotheses

Three-quarters of all mermaid sightings occur in waters where no seals or sea cows live. How can we explain these sightings? Cryptozoologists propose that mermaids are creatures that have not yet been discovered.

Cryptozoology

Cryptozoology is the search for animals whose existence has not been proven, such as Bigfoot, unicorns, or mermaids. To strengthen their case, cryptozoologists point to the recent discovery of the megamouth shark. This 1,653-pound (750-kilogram), 15-foot- (4.5-meter-) long fish was completely unknown until members of the U.S. Navy pulled it from the bottom of the sea in 1976. Its discovery makes us wonder: What other undiscovered creatures could lurk in our waters?

▼ Until 1976, no one knew this huge fish, the megamouth shark, even existed. What other sea creatures will we discover in our oceans?

But is cryptozoology a "real" science?

Most scientists do not recognize cryptozoology as an official branch of science. Although scientists agree that thousands of unknown animals exist—particularly insects—they criticize cryptozoologists for focusing their efforts mostly on exciting and elusive (hard to find) creatures, like mermaids, despite little scientific support for their existence. But cryptozoologists point out that many real animals, including giant pandas, were once believed to only exist in myths.

▼ Female divers in Korea and Japan collected seafood deep in the ocean. Visitors might have mistaken these women for mermaids.

Haenyo divers

In 1653, Dutch sailor Hendrik Hamel encountered a violent storm off the coast of Korea that wrecked his ship and drowned half of his passengers. Hamel managed to swim to Cheju, a Korean island—and that is where he saw mermaids.

Although his account was met with disbelief, scientists now agree that these "mermaids" were probably Haenyo divers. These are Korean women who hold their breath while diving deep into the sea to gather seafood. European women at the time rarely swam—and when they did, they covered their bodies from head to toe. So, to a Dutch sailor, the Haenyo divers—who swam in little or no clothing—must have seemed like a completely new species!

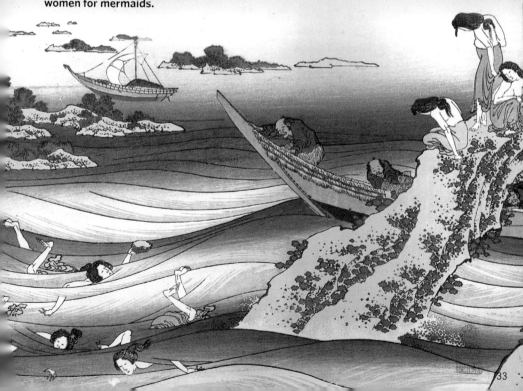

Mistakes and Hoaxes

Some mermaid sightings may be cases of mistaken identity with other creatures. But others are the result of deliberate hoaxes.

The monkey mermaid

When American sea captain Samuel Eades arrived in the Caribbean Islands in 1822, he saw a mermaid body for sale. Although it was ugly— with a dry, shriveled face, claws, and a scaly fish tail—Eades wanted to own it. He could not afford the $6,000 price tag, so sold his ship and all the cargo in it to purchase the creature. Eades figured he would earn back all of his money by exhibiting the mermaid in London, England.

Back in London, a famous naturalist examined the creature and declared that mermaids really did exist! So Eades displayed the mermaid in a popular coffee shop, where 400 people a day paid for a glimpse of the creature.

But soon a respected scientist revealed that the "mermaid" was actually a fake—it was the body of a female orangutan that had been skillfully wired to the tail of a salmon. Eades continued to display the mermaid, but the public soon lost interest. Meanwhile, Eades spent the rest of his life working for his shipping company, trying to pay back his debt.

Making the fakes

Captain Eades's fake mermaid was not the first fake, and it would not be the last. During the 1700s and 1800s, skilled craftspeople and fishermen in Japan and the Caribbean Islands made a lot of money by creating fake mermaids, which they exhibited, used in religious ceremonies, and sold to Dutch traders. Fishermen also claimed that these mermaids had warned them that big floods were coming, and that only a mermaid amulet (good luck charm) could ward off destruction—and, of course, they had amulets to sell as well.

▲ The "mermaid" on this carving resembles the type created by many Japanese craftsmen.

▲ In the 1700s and 1800s, some people were fooled by "mermaids" made from the bodies of monkeys attached to fish tails, like this one.

Many people who saw the mermaid were disappointed, since the shriveled creature looked nothing like the beautiful mermaid drawings that Barnum used to advertise the show.

The "Fiji mermaid"

Samuel Eades's mermaid got a second life in 1842, when P. T. Barnum, the American showman and founder of the Barnum and Bailey Circus, rented the mermaid from the Boston Museum. He named it the "Fiji mermaid," telling people it had been captured in the Fiji Islands, and he displayed it in his new museum, Scudder's American Museum, in New York City.

The "Great Chain of Being" theory

By 1842, few scientists still believed in mermaids, but the public was less sure. When Barnum's museum opened, crowds poured in to see the mermaid and listen as a professor named Dr. Griffin explained his "Great Chain of Being" theory. He declared that God had created an unlimited chain of animals—everything from pigs to pigeons to mermaids—in order from the simplest to the most complex. The mermaid, Griffin argued, was a link between man and fish, just as the flying fish was a link between birds and fish. He also claimed that all things on land have a match in the sea. Since there were sea lions and sea horses, why not sea humans?

But Dr. Griffin was not a scientist at all. He was Barnum's assistant, and he was hired to fool people. His "links" had no basis in science. For example, flying fish leap out of the water using fins—not wings. They have no connection to birds. And sea horses are simply tiny fish with horse-shaped heads. They are not related to horses.

Many people who saw the mermaid were disappointed, since the shriveled creature looked nothing like the beautiful mermaid drawings that Barnum used to advertise the show. However, the creature's ugliness convinced others it was real. They felt that reality often fails to live up to fantasy.

▼ Both Samuel Eades and P. T. Barnum tried to convince the public that this creature, often called the "Fiji mermaid," was real.

Etched by Geo Cruikshank

Pub by G Humphrey 27 St James's St London
Octr 20th 1822

The Mermaid!

Now Exhibiting at the Turf Coffee-house 39 St James's Street.

The merman of Cornwall

As villagers strolled along the high cliffs of Bude, on the coast of Cornwall, England, in 1825, they heard a haunting melody wafting up from the shores below. A full moon spotlighted the source of the music: a figure, perched on the rocks near the shore. It had long, brown hair, entangled with seaweed, the milky-white chest of a man, and the tail of a fish. After belting out several songs, the merman dived into the sea.

Night after night, the merman reappeared, always singing and braiding his long, flowing locks. Soon people from neighboring towns flocked to Bude to get a glimpse of the mysterious man-fish. Then, one night, after performing a slightly hoarse version of the British national anthem, "God Save the King," the merman plunged into the sea, never to return.

The villagers were all abuzz with excitement— except for Robert Hawker, the town vicar (local priest). Fascinated with mermaids, he had fooled the villagers, whom he considered superstitious (believing in illogical things), by pretending to be the merman. He had worn a wig of seaweed and wrapped his legs in oilskins. But after a few weeks, his voice grew scratchy, and he grew cold from sitting so long near the water. That is when he ended the hoax. Many years later, Hawker confessed his prank to leaders at his church.

The tsunami mermaid

After a tsunami hit the coast of India in 2004, the Internet was flooded with e-mails claiming that the waves had washed something amazing to shore—the body of a mermaid! There was even a photo. But when researchers checked, they were unable to find the original source for the e-mail. And the photo was traced back to 2003, when it had been used in another mermaid e-mail hoax.

▲ Several photographs showing creatures that look like mermaids circulate the Internet every year. Some of them are shown here. What do you think?

Filipino fraud

In February 2009, several radio stations in the city of Dumaguete, in the Philippines, announced some astonishing news. A mermaid had washed ashore nearby and had been taken to a laboratory at Silliman University for study. Within minutes, a crowd had gathered in front of the lab. The security guards at the facility explained that the rumor was false—there was no mermaid inside. But dozens of citizens insisted on purchasing passes from the university to enter the lab, only to discover that it was a hoax!

A model mermaid

What about the mysterious 1967 mermaid sighted near Victoria, Canada (see page 16)? What did observers really see? A photograph published in the local paper the next day showed a woman with long, blonde locks, a smiling face, and a tapered mermaid tail. The mermaid soon became the talk of the town, and the local aquarium offered a $25,000 reward for its safe capture.

Just a few days later, it seemed that some members of a local sports club had won the reward, when they were spotted carrying the mermaid near a bay about 20 miles (32 kilometers) away. However, on closer inspection, it was obvious that this "mermaid" was only a plastic dummy. This same dummy was probably used to trick the passengers near Victoria. The reason for the hoax is unclear, although it did draw attention to the town.

▼ A mermaid spotted near this Vancouver Island lighthouse was discovered to be only a plastic dummy.

Mystery mermaid

The 2009 mermaid sightings near Kiryat Yam, Israel (see pages 16 and 17), also drew attention to the region. But interest gradually faded when the sightings stopped and no one claimed the $1 million reward. The sightings are still a mystery, although some people have accused local businesses of "hiring" a mermaid to create headlines, excitement, and tourism.

▼ Some believe that the town of Kiryat Yam, Israel, tried to boost tourism by hiring a professional mermaid model, such as Hannah Fraser (pictured), to pose as a mermaid.

Why We Believe

Have we solved the mystery of mermaids? Although lots of people claim to have spotted mermaids, many of these sightings may be cases of mistaken identity with other sea creatures. Others can be explained by hoaxes. Some can be attributed to wishful thinking or exaggeration. Others are still unexplained. But to prove that mermaids exist, more evidence is needed, such as fossils or bones from mermaids or even reliable photographs. So far, no scientific proof for mermaids has been found.

Science cannot prove that mermaids exist, but the investigation has revealed how powerful our desire is to believe. Why else would we create hoaxes—or fall for them? Why else would we mistake big, bald sea creatures for mermaids? And why else would we tell so many stories about mermaids? Mermaids may not exist in reality, but they continue to feed our imaginations.

Water, water everywhere

Water covers most of Earth, but it contains many mysteries and dangers. It helps us live, but also harms us. Stormy seas can flood towns and sink ships. Mermaid myths can help us feel powerful against nature's mood swings. For instance, if we believe sirens cause shipwrecks, we can try to steer clear of these charming but dangerous sea creatures.

▼ Legends of Syrian goddess Atargatis, a half-woman, half-fish ruler of the seas, date back to at least 4000 BCE.

Modern mermaid myth:
The Little Mermaid

Many people are familiar with Disney's version of *The Little Mermaid*, but fewer people know the original story by Hans Christian Andersen. In Andersen's tale, the mermaid gives up her tail and her beautiful singing voice in the hopes of gaining the love of a human prince. But she ends up with nothing at all. Although the story is sad, it is a valuable reminder to young people never to give up the gifts that make them unique in order to gain the affection of another.

Timeline

8th century BCE
The *Odyssey* is written, recounting tales of dangerous sirens who lure sailors to ruin.

337 CE
A 195-foot (60-meter) "mermaid" is caught off the coast of Scotland. It is probably a whale.

early 1400s
The "Edam mermaid" is discovered in Lake Purmer, in Holland.

1410
Pierre d'Ailly claims in his book *Imago Mundi* that strange creatures inhabit the "New World."

1493
Christopher Columbus reports seeing three mermaids jumping out of the water near the coast of Haiti.

1608
Explorer Henry Hudson reports seeing a mermaid near Russia.

1610
British sea captain Richard Whitbourne reports that a mermaid off the coast of Newfoundland approached him at the shore.

1614
English sea captain John Smith reports seeing an attractive mermaid near the Caribbean coast.

1700s and 1800s
Fishermen and craftspeople in Japan and the Caribbean create fake mermaids.

1718
A creature is caught off the island of Borneo.

1811
Catherine Loynachan and John McIsaac both observe an unusual part-boy, part-fish creature near the rocky shore of Corphin, Scotland.

1822
American sea captain Samuel Eades displays the body of a mermaid in London. It is later proved to be a stuffed orangutan and salmon wired together.

1825
Robert Hawker poses as a merman off the coast of Cornwall, England, fooling nearby villagers.

1842
P. T. Barnum displays the "Fiji mermaid" in New York City.

1893
The hunting of sea cows is banned.

1967
A group of passengers aboard a ferryboat near Vancouver Island, Canada, claims to spot a mermaid. Days later, it is revealed to be a hoax.

2004
After a tsunami hits India, an e-mail claims that a mermaid washed ashore. But the e-mail and photo are discovered to be hoaxes.

2009
A radio station in the Philippines spreads a false rumor that a mermaid had washed ashore.

People on the beach near Kiryat Yam, Israel, report regular appearances by a mermaid at sunset.

Summing Up the Science

People have proposed all sorts of unusual hypotheses to explain mermaid sightings. Let's see how some of them stand up to science.

Hypothesis	The science
Mermaids are related to aliens from outer space who settled areas of Earth deep under the ocean and eventually mated with fish.	This hypothesis is "out there." No evidence exists to support it.
Creatures that closely resembled mermaids once existed but are now extinct or rare. For instance, a now-extinct species of sea cows might have been mistaken for mermaids.	If true, this hypothesis would only prove the existence of a different type of sea cow, not mermaids. Plus, it would not explain recent mermaid sightings.
Mermaids once existed but are now extinct.	No "mermaid" fossils have yet been found.

Mermaid mythology: The angry merman

Long ago, a mermaid wept bitter tears as she struggled to escape a fisherman's net. As villagers from the busy port town of Westenschouwen, in Holland, gathered around the mermaid, a low, rumbling voice arose from the waves. It was a merman, commanding the fishermen to return his wife to the sea. When the fishermen ignored his pleas, the merman bellowed: "Westenschouwen, you'll regret this all your life, that you have robbed me of my wife. The town will drown and lose its power. The only remains will be its tower." The villagers turned a deaf ear, and soon the entire town was flooded. Only the watchtower remained.

This, of course, is only a legend. But like most legends, it serves an important purpose—to provide a lesson or an explanation for a mysterious or scary real-life event. The fact that mermaid stories and sightings have occurred in nearly every country and culture does not prove that mermaids are real. But it does show that humans have a strong desire or need to believe in merfolk.

Glossary

aquatic something that grows or lives in or near the water

cetacean class of large aquatic mammals, including whales, dolphins, and porpoises, with hairless bodies and broad flippers

cryptozoologist researcher who studies and searches for animals whose existence has not yet been confirmed

cryptozoology study of and search for animals whose existence has not yet been confirmed

descend come from a common ancestor

dugong large, plant-eating aquatic mammal with paddle-shaped tails and flipper-like forelimbs that lives in the warm coastal waters of the Indian Ocean near Africa and northern Australia

evidence facts or information that help show whether or not a belief or theory is true

evolution gradual development of something, from a simple to a more complex form

exhibit display for others to see

fossil remains or imprint (in a bone, shell, or rock) of a living creature from another time period

hoax a trick

hypothesis explanation for an occurrence or problem that needs evidence or testing before it can be accepted as true

legend frequently told story that is not necessarily supported by fact

mammal warm-blooded animal that produces milk for its young

manatee large, plant-eating aquatic mammal with paddle-like front flippers and a spoon-shaped tail that lives in the warm coastal waters of Florida, South America, West Africa, and the Caribbean

myth ancient or traditional story, usually involving superhuman beings, that often explains customs or natural events

naturalist person who studies nature

porpoise member of the whale family, it is similar to a dolphin but smaller in size, with a blunt spout and a triangular fin

scientific method process of investigation in which a problem or question is identified, and then experiments are conducted or evidence is found to solve the problem or answer the question

selkie creature in Irish and Scottish folklore that looks like a seal

siren part-bird, part-woman creature from Greek mythology whose singing lured sailors onto the rocks where she lived, so that she could then devour them

sirenian order of aquatic, plant-eating mammals with paddle-like forelimbs and a flattened tail. The group consists of dugongs and manatees, and they are also referred to as sea cows.

species group of living beings that share some common traits and are capable of interbreeding with each other

theory explanation of some aspect of the natural world that is supported by evidence

tsunami large, high ocean wave caused by an underwater earthquake or volcanic eruption

Find Out More

Books

Andersen, Hans Christian. *The Little Mermaid*. New York: Penguin, 2004 (originally published 1837).

Berk, Ari. *The Secret History of Mermaids and Creatures of the Deep*. Somerville, Mass.: Candlewick, 2009.

Dunmore, Helen. *Ingo*. New York: HarperCollins, 2006.

Guillain, Charlotte. *Mermaids* (Mythical Creatures). Chicago: Raintree, 2011.

Knudsen, Shannon. *Mermaids and Mermen* (Fantasy Chronicles). Minneapolis: Lerner, 2010.

Osborne, Mary Pope. *Mermaid Tales from Around the World*. New York: Scholastic, 1999.

Web sites

www.mermaid.net/mermaid
Find out more of the history and mythology of mermaids.

www.newanimal.org/merfolk.htm
This offers a short history of mermaids as well as links to additional resources.

www.savethemanatee.org/manfcts.htm
Find information about manatees and how to help save this endangered species.

www.sirenian.org/sirenians.html
Find information about both manatees and dugongs and how you can help save these endangered species.

Films

The Little Mermaid: Aquamarine (20th Century Fox, 2006)
Two best friends get exactly what they are fishing for in this comedy about friendship.

The Secret of Roan Inish (Columbia Tristar, 1995; 2000)
Ten-year-old Fiona, sent to live with her grandparents in a small Irish fishing village, learns that a relative of hers married a selkie (seal woman). Can the selkies save her baby brother, who has disappeared into the sea?

Splash! (Buena Vista Home Entertainment, 1984; 2004)
A young businessman is rescued from a boating accident by the girl of his dreams. But she is not like other women!

Index